Facebook Marketing Solutions

The Facebook Advertising Solution

[O. Addey]

Copyright © 2021 **O. Addey**

All rights reserved.

Table of Contents

Introduction 6
Chapter-02: Facebook Marketing 8
   Why is Facebook good for marketing? 8
   Formats of Facebook Marketing 10
Chapter-02: Facebook Marketing strategy 14
   Choose the best timing 14
   Promote your Facebook page on other channels. 15
   Use a relevant URL for your page 15
   Add a CTA button. 15
   Support customers via a Facebook Messenger bot.
   16
   Use a Facebook pixel 16
   Create lookalike audiences 16
   What can Facebook add to email marketing? 17
   How can email marketing combine with Facebook?
   17
Chapter -03: How to Set Up a Facebook Page 18
   Create a Facebook Page 18
      Add a Profile Picture 19
      Add a Cover Photo 19
      Add a Short Description 20

Create a Username for Your Page 20
    Add Your Page to Shortcuts 20
    Set Up Page Roles 21
Customize Your Notifications 22
Add a Page CTA 22
    Organize Your Page Tabs 23
    Verify Your Page 23
Chapter-04: Tracking and Measuring Results with Facebook Analytics 24
    Using Page Insights 24
    Likes 25
    Reach 25
    Page Views 25
    Posts 26
    Post Details 26
    Facebook Reactions 27
    Measuring Social ROI 27
Chapter-05: How to Advertise on Facebook 29
    How to Create a Facebook Ad Campaign 29
    How to Target and Optimize Ad Sets 30
        Daily Budget: 31
        Lifetime Budget: 31

    Facebook Ad Formats 31

    Measuring Facebook Ad Results 32

        Actions: 32

        Cost per action: 33

        Frequency: 33

Chapter-06: How to Create an Effective Facebook Marketing Strategy 34

    Step 1. Set your goals 34

    Step 2. Define your target audience 35

    Step 3. Choose content formats and schedule posts 36

    Step 4. Boost your post with Facebook Ads 37

    Step 5. Make use of Facebook tools 38

        Facebook Messenger 38

        Pages to Watch 39

        Invite Engaged Users 39

    Step 6: Measure your effectiveness 40

Conclusion 41

Introduction

Facebook is the most popular social media site, with two billion people using it every month. However, if you want your business to stand out among the 50 million companies on Facebook, you'll need an effective Facebook marketing plan! Many small companies' marketing tactics revolve around Facebook advertising. However, in addition to your advertisements, you must pay attention to the content on your page. Facebook marketing is a system that offers a variety of highly targeted paid advertising and organic postings, allowing businesses to promote their products and services to a large audience. As a result, Facebook has evolved from the most significant social medium to one of the largest markets over the previous decade.

Facebook is not a new concept, nor is the notion that every business needs a Facebook page. However, a great deal has changed since Facebook first joined the marketing landscape. Today, the world's largest social network can accomplish things that many of us could never have imagined ten years ago, such as hosting 360-degree films, selling items through a chatbot, and even serving as the primary news source for two-thirds of the adults' population. Facebook has 1.56 billion active users daily. Let's put things in context. That's roughly five times the population of the United States or 20% of the world's population... and it is still rising. Consider the social impact that Facebook may provide in terms of peer effects, eCommerce business, referrals, customer connections, reputation, brand recognition, and much more (let alone, in combination with other social media platforms you market through). Not only does Facebook have a large number of users, but it also has a large portion of our attention. Globally, the average Facebook user spends about an hour each day on the platform. The typical person sleeps eight hours each day, so this equates to around 7% of our waking hours spent with our eyes riveted to the social network.

Chapter-02: Facebook Marketing

Why is Facebook good for marketing?

1. Has worldwide coverage
2. Provides highly tailored sponsored advertisements
3. Allows for organic reach
4. Integration with various marketing channels is possible.
5. The Advantages of Facebook Marketing
6. Exact targeting
7. Boosted website traffic Various ad types
8. Customer service
9. Positive effects on SEO

In this part, we'll go deeper into the benefits of using Facebook in your marketing plan. Aside from reaching a large audience, you'll learn what other goals you may achieve with this platform.

Precise targeting

You're probably aware that Facebook allows users to segment their audiences carefully, but let's take a deeper look at the choices available. You may choose an audience based on their income, education level, life events, relationship status, or employment inside demographic targeting. You may seek consumers by considering their interests, such as their favorite forms of entertainment, sports, hobbies, and purchasing patterns. You may also reach out to clients depending on their purchasing habits, intent, device usage, and so on.

Increased website traffic

You may send your viewers to your website using this platform. Furthermore, because they already know your organization, these folks will be higher quality leads than users who come on your site organically. As a result, you have greater credibility in their eyes. Encourage your followers to go to your website to learn more about your products. In addition, when you connect to a website, Facebook generates a full-size image if your page has one. As a result, it will pique the interest of many users and assist you in increasing website traffic.

Variety of ad formats

Facebook offers fantastic chances for businesses to exhibit their items from the finest viewpoints. This platform's advertisements come in both text and graphic formats. You may promote your post by converting it into an ad, creating tales to highlight your behind-the-scenes, creating a slideshow of your new collection, and using carousel advertisements to showcase up to ten goods connecting to the appropriate pages so on.

Customer support

Many consumers prefer to interact with a company through social media. Phone calls are becoming obsolete. Set up A Facebook Messenger chatbot to engage with people based on the keywords they frequently ask. They can contain terms like "pricing," "delivery," "payment choices," "buy," "book," and so on. You simply need to create a scenario based on FAQs from users and provide the responses. Your chatbot will mimic the real-world dialogue. Consequently, your support personnel will have more time to work on more complex issues, and you will be able to automate regular activities.

Positive impact on SEO

Some marketers argue that social media has an impact on search engine results. It is thought that while ranking, robots take your information in the About section into account. Furthermore, your social media participation is very important. Shares, likes, and comments show Google that people are interested in and engaged with your brand. Although there is no specific proof, it is also not superfluous.

Formats of Facebook Marketing

1. Video ad
2. Image ads
3. Carousel ads
4. Collection ad

5. Slideshow ads
6. Lead generation ads

Facebook is not just a social media giant, but it is also a rapidly expanding corporation, with half a million new accounts established every day. As time passes, Facebook engineers create new ad formats to match the contemporary requirements of Facebook Advertisements funnel development while improving time-tested ads. Here's a rundown of the many Facebook marketing formats:

Video ad

It's a great method to show off your product's features in action. In addition, Facebook permits the use of several forms of video to achieve certain purposes, such as short films and GIFs to rapidly catch attention on the go or In-Stream videos for extended TV-like viewing.

Image ads

If your budget does not allow you to create a video, an image ad is an excellent option for quickly and easily generating a high-quality commercial. In addition, this approach will assist you in increasing brand recognition and driving traffic to your website.

Carousel ads

This style enables the display of up to 10 pictures or videos within single advertising, each linked to a distinct product page. Because you may highlight one product in-depth, a few distinct goods, or construct a tale divided by those carousel cards, it opens up a huge area for creativity and engagement.

Collection ad

It's like a mini-catalog of your items in the form of a Facebook post. For example, a Collection ad comprises one original video or image and four smaller images arranged in a grid below.

Slideshow ads

It is a video-like format that shows well even when the internet connection speed is slow. You may make such an ad utilizing several stock pictures, video editing software, and even music.

Lead generation ads

This format was created to aid in the generation of leads, particularly for mobile users. When a user taps on the picture in such an advertisement, a subscription form appears right in the ad, allowing them to opt-in to your newsletters with only a few taps.

In addition, there are three sorts of ads for promoting interaction: post engagement, event replies, and page likes.

Chapter-02: Facebook Marketing strategy

1. Facebook Marketing Tips
2. Choose the best timing
3. Promote your Facebook page on other channels
4. Use a relevant URL for your page
5. Add a CTA button
6. Support customers via a Facebook Messenger bot
7. Use a Facebook pixel
8. Create lookalike audiences

There are several hacks available to assist you in improving the effectiveness of your Facebook marketing approach. We'll go through a few pointers in this section.

Choose the best timing

Marketers are always looking for the best time to release their products. There is no one-size-fits-all solution, but Facebook Insights may provide useful information. You may discover information about when your followers are online in this section. You may also examine the performance of every post to determine the ideal time to publish it. You also learn when your audience is most engaged. Furthermore, you may experiment and upload different types of content during peak and non-peak periods to determine the best timing.

Promote your Facebook page on other channels.

To increase traffic to your page, make sure that as many of your potential consumers as possible are aware of it. You are almost certainly active on other digital marketing platforms, so why should you pass up this opportunity? For example, add a Facebook button to each of your email marketing campaigns so that users may quickly click the link. If you use Instagram, you may include a link to your Facebook profile in your bio. If you run a blog, allow users to share content with their Facebook connections.

Use a relevant URL for your page.

This aspect may not appear to be as essential as it is. We imply utilizing your brand name in a relevant URL. You will be able to share your link on other channels quickly, it will be easier to distinguish and remember, and you will appear more professional. The most significant advantage is that your URL will include your keyword, which will improve your SEO strategy and make your website more searchable on Google.

Add a CTA button.

This simple method will assist you in increasing conversions, increasing engagement, and driving traffic to any website. Your aim determines everything. Examine your website and consider what action a typical visitor may wish to do after viewing it. It may be "Contact Us," "Sign up," "Book now," "Shop Now," "Follow," "Call now," and so on. To add a CTA, go to your cover page and select "+Add a Button."

Support customers via a Facebook Messenger bot.

Customers want brands to respond quickly. Manually doing this is a difficult process. Create a chatbot to answer FAQs, assist consumers with orders, identify delivery difficulties, and just learn more about your company. Without any technological knowledge, you can develop a chatbot for Facebook Messenger with SendPulse. You simply need to use terms to construct conversational logic.

Use a Facebook pixel.

This is an analytics tool that gives you additional information about your clients' actions. For example, you may create highly targeted advertising for future campaigns using a Facebook pixel. You may also track the efficacy of your advertisements. For example, when a user makes a purchase or performs another activity, it is recorded. Consequently, you can determine whether your advertising is producing the desired results and then use Custom Audience to reach out to this customer.

Create lookalike audiences.

This is an excellent approach to reach out to new Facebook audiences. These people do not know your brand but might become consumers since they are comparable to your present customers. You can develop a successful Facebook marketing plan and supplement it with SendPulse chatbots with these helpful hints.

What can Facebook add to email marketing?

Facebook allows users to sign up for your email newsletters right from a Facebook post with Lead advertising. Aside from Lead advertising, you can use positive user feedback gathered on Facebook into your email marketing to boost the sense of trust using social proof. Try SendPulse's Facebook connection to ensure that all people that subscribe to your Facebook page are automatically included in your mailing list.

How can email marketing combine with Facebook?

Email marketing is a platform in which the core communication unit is an email – a message including content, offers, and calls-to-action. Its goal is to increase sales and establish long-term relationships with the audience. You may include social media icons in the footer of each email and encourage readers to interact with your company on Facebook. You may also send out giveaway emails with incentives for sharing your business on social media. With SendPulse, you can gather customers' email addresses while also allowing them to join your chatbot on Facebook Messenger using a single signup form. You must provide a link to your chatbot to build a multichannel form.

Chapter -03: How to Set Up a Facebook Page

You've made the proper decision if you've decided to create a Facebook Page for your company. In reality, you'll be joining the 70 million companies worldwide that currently market using a Facebook Page, a figure that has increased by 1 million in the previous few years. So let's go back to the beginning and work through the setup procedure before we get into publishing content and boosting pieces with advertising.

Create a Facebook Page

As you may be aware, the vast bulk of Facebook is made up of personal accounts. If you are a company seeking to build a presence on the social network, you must instead create a Page. Pages are Facebook's answer to a business profile. Pages resemble profile pages but include information relevant to businesses, groups, and causes. You connect with a business Facebook Page by "liking" it and becoming a fan instead of adding a profile as a friend. If you create a personal profile for your business instead of a Page, Facebook may deactivate it.

Facebook provides two categories to let you modify the fields on your page. Let's pretend we're a "Business or Brand" for the sake of this introduction. When you click "Get Started," you will be led to add a Profile Photo and Cover Photo to your new page. (You may skip these steps and complete them later, but we encourage doing so now.) If you skip, you'll see your new Facebook Page as well as a few ideas for laying the groundwork for a business Page.

Add a Profile Picture

The first step in giving your Facebook Page a personality is to upload a profile photo. This will be your page's primary graphic, showing in search results and with any of your content that appears in a user's News Feed. Most publishers recommend generating a photo with a resolution of 180 × 180 pixels, although raising this slightly will assist retain quality. If you do not submit a picture that is already square, you will be asked to crop it.

Consider your profile image to be your initial impression, and make sure to select something instantly identifiable (like a logo). If you're a public personality or a speaker, use a preferred headshot. Local restaurants and stores may select a picture of their most popular item.

Add a Cover Photo

Following that, Facebook will recommend that you add a cover photo. The huge, horizontal image that covers the top of your page is known as a cover photo. It should represent your page's personality and be modified frequently based on special offers, promotions, or seasons. To add a cover photo, go to the welcome menu and select "Add a Cover Photo." A cover photo's official specifications are 851 x 315 pixels. If your photo isn't just right, you'll be able to reposition it by dragging. Finally, click the "Save" button.

Add a Short Description

Your page is coming up nicely, with some lovely pictures. Then you'll need a description to tell your audience what your company is all about. To begin, click "Add a Short Description" beneath "Welcome to Your New Page." Next, add one to two sentences (or a maximum of 255 characters) about your company. This description will display on your page and in search results, so keep it brief yet descriptive. But don't be scared to exhibit a little individuality with your brand!

Create a Username for Your Page

The final step in the welcome menu is to give your page a username. To help people locate and remember your page, your username will show in your unique Facebook URL (also known as a vanity URL). You'll have 50 characters to come up with a unique name that isn't already in use by another company.

Add Your Page to Shortcuts

We've completed the four steps from Facebook's welcome menu, but there are a few more things you can do to personalize your page. Every Facebook user, for example, has a vertical navigation bar to the left of their News Feed. You'll always have fast access to your page if you add it as a shortcut here. To make it easier to get to your page in the future, go to your News Feed and click on "Edit" next to "Shortcuts" in the left vertical menu.

Set Up Page Roles

After you've completed the basic skeleton of your page, there's one more step you'll want to do before sending it out to the world... or even your coworkers. Remember how Facebook generates separate business Pages from personal profiles? One advantage is that several employees inside an organization may update and post to the page without sharing login information. However, you must also specify who has what degrees of editing access. This is where Page Roles come into play.

Admin: Admins may control all page elements, including sending messages, publishing as the page, responding to or deleting comments, creating advertisements, seeing who published a certain post, and assigning Page responsibilities. This individual would have the same permissions as the page's creator. Make an informed decision.

Editor: Editors have the same privileges as Admins, with one major exception: Editors cannot give Page roles to other users.

Moderator: Moderators can send messages, react to and remove comments, but they cannot publish as the page. They do have the ability to make advertisements.

Advertiser: Advertisers may create advertisements and view insights, just as it sounds.

Analysts have no publishing authority, but they can check whose administrator published a given post and examine insights.

Jobs Manager: Jobs Managers get access to all of the same features as Advertisers and the ability to publish and manage jobs.

Customize Your Notifications

While in the settings menu, navigate to "Notifications." This area allows you to personalize how you get alerts for Page activity. For example, you may opt to receive a notification every time there is the action or only once every 12 to 24 hours.

Add a Page CTA

One of the most significant advantages of having a Facebook Page for your business is the potential to reach an audience that a traditional website would not have been able to reach. The average buyer's journey, however, does not conclude on Facebook. Beginning in December 2014, Facebook Pages might incorporate a call-to-action button at the top of their page. To make one, go to the bottom of your cover photo, and select "+ Add a Button." You may select from various options depending on whether you want to browse or book a service, contact someone, make a purchase or contribution, download an app, or simply learn more.

Organize Your Page Tabs

Do you want to take your company's page to the next level? Create custom tabs to customize the content that people view when they visit your page. When you visit Starbucks' Page, for example, you may browse images, view open positions, visit its Pinterest account, or discover a location near you. Go to "Settings" > "Templates and Tabs" to alter the tabs on your page. You have the option of using Facebook's default tabs or adding new ones. You may also build a custom app using the Facebook Developer site.

Verify Your Page

You may be qualified for a verification badge based on how you classified your page. A blue label indicates that Facebook has verified the authenticity of a prominent figure, media company, or brand's page. The Agiary badge indicates that Facebook has verified the authenticity of a company or organization's Page. First, check if your page has a profile image and a cover photo to see whether you're eligible. Next, navigate to "Settings" > "General." There, you may input your publicly posted phone number, country, and language under "Page Verification." You will be contacted by phone and given a verification code.

Chapter-04: Tracking and Measuring Results with Facebook Analytics

You have put in a lot of effort to get your Facebook Page up and running. You've given your Page individuality with photos and language, pondered unique methods to acquire likes, and created a content plan that appeals to your target demographic. So, how did you fare? Unfortunately, without a framework for tracking and assessing results, Facebook marketing will result in much guessing and, eventually, underperformance. Fortunately, Facebook has created a thorough Page Insights tool to assist you in analyzing your page as a whole and drilling down on particular articles.

Using Page Insights

Page Insights can be accessed by selecting "Insights" from the menu at the top of your page. There, you'll be taken to the "Overview" area, which provides a seven-day summary of the essential activity on your page. (Because my example Page is very new, the metrics are sparse.) Next, you'll notice several tabs in the left vertical navigation bar to see various parts of your Page analytics. Finally, we'll go through the important tabs to look at while reporting on your Facebook Page in this section.

Likes

First, look at the "Likes" tab. You can check how many likes you got or lost each day in this section.

On the "Net Likes" graph, the number of new likes minus the number of unlikes daily may be seen. Click and drag the graph to narrow down the date range. You may also compare your average performance over time by using the "Benchmark" feature on the right side.

Reach

The "Reach" option displays the number of people who saw your content, divided by organic and sponsored traffic. Remember that the more likes, comments, and shares a post receive, the higher it appears in the News Feed. Similarly, the more individuals who hide a message or label it as spam, the less likely it appears in the News Feed. So, if you observe a surge in reach on a certain day, click on that point on the graph to see the exact content and take note of how people engaged.

Page Views

Page Views" assists you in determining how people arrived at your page and where they go once there. Next, examine the "Top Sources" graph to see which external referrers bring you the most traffic. It's most likely your website, blog, or search engine.

Posts

The "Posts" tab in Page Insights is most likely the most useful. At the top, you'll see a graph that shows when your fans are online. This may be quite beneficial when you create your social media content plan and schedule posts. In addition, this section contains a list of all your published posts in reverse chronological order, as well as their key stats. Keep an eye on this chart not just to measure your progress but also to discover what sorts of content your audience prefers.

To access Page Insights, go to the menu at the top of your page and select "Insights." Then select whatever metrics you want to display in the graphic. For example, if you pick the "Engagement Rate" view, you may notice a high-performing organic article. This is a nice post to think about boosting with paid advertising.

Post Details

While Page Insights is fantastic for monthly reports, there are times when you want to browse your page and check how a single article is performing. You can access post information without navigating to Page Insights by clicking on the "people reached" number just above the "Like" button. This is where you can get more detailed stats for video content, such as 10-second views and average viewing time.

Facebook Reactions

In February 2016, Facebook introduced a new function called "Reactions" to users worldwide. Users have "like" anything provided by both personal accounts and Pages for many years. Users may now express their love, rage, laughing, and other emotions. For the time being, Facebook Reactions are treated the same as likes. However, by viewing the Post Details, you may examine the breakdown of reactions on a certain post. Thanks to the advent of Reactions, marketers now have a better understanding of what their audience thinks of their content. People who "love" your content are likely to be good brand advocates. Also, keep in mind that an "angry" person may not detest the substance but rather the subject matter.

Measuring Social ROI

You want to know that the time you spend establishing and managing your Facebook page is worthwhile. That is why calculating your social return on investment is critical.

Before attempting to measure your ROI, you must first establish goals. Views, engagement, lead generation, or a mix of these might be key performance metrics. Then, every time you share a link to Facebook, remember to utilize tracking URLs with UTM parameters. Then, using a marketing automation tool like HubSpot, you can build these links right in the program, attach them to a campaign, and measure how many clicks contribute to your total view and lead objectives. Finally, the closed-loop reporting supplied by marketing automation software can assist you in determining whether social media posts are truly influencing the business's bottom line - in terms of leads and consumers. As a result, you may be more confident in your judgments and gain greater support from executives for your social activities.

Chapter-05: How to Advertise on Facebook

When you first start advertising on Facebook, you may feel as if you have many boxes to complete. Is your copy interesting enough? Are you reaching out to the appropriate people? What should I spend my money on?

Unfortunately, the overwhelming nature of Facebook advertising discourages many people from even attempting it. However, with such a large and diversified user base, Facebook presents a unique opportunity for marketers to raise brand recognition. This opportunity may potentially result in more leads for your company than any other paid channel. We'll guide you through the steps to get started with Facebook advertising, ensuring you're creating the appropriate ad at the right moment.

How to Create a Facebook Ad Campaign

Understanding the terms is the first step in the Facebook advertising checklist. All sponsored advertising on Facebook may be divided into three categories:

Campaigns: A campaign is where you keep all of your assets.

Ad sets: Ad sets are collections of advertising that are targeted towards certain audiences. If you're trying to reach out to numerous audiences, you'll need to create unique sets for each.

Ads: Individual advertising that you will post on Facebook, each with its colors, wording, photos, and so on.

When you create your first advertising on Facebook, you have two editors to choose from: the Ad Manager and the Power Editor. The Ad Manager is ideal for most businesses, but the Power Editor was designed for bigger advertisers who want exact management over a range of campaigns. Therefore, we'll utilize the Ad Manager for these instructions. To access the Facebook Ads Manager, go to your homepage and select "Ads Manager" from the left-hand menu. Before you can develop an ad, you must first decide on an aim. Facebook offers 11 options, divided into three categories: awareness, contemplation, and conversion.

How to Target and Optimize Ad Sets

Once you've chosen an aim for your campaign, Facebook will guide you through a few stages to establish your ad set's audience, budget, and timeline. If you've already utilized Facebook's advertising capabilities, you may choose a stored audience here. Alternatively, provide demographic information such as location, age, gender, and language.

You may then refine your targeting in the detailed targeting box. Choose one of Facebook's pre-made categories or enter the name of a specific company Page that your target audience may have liked. You can, for example, target women's clothes fans and customers of the retailer Anthropologie.

Keep the "Automatic Placements (Recommended)" option selected in the "Placements" section.

Then decide on a budget and a timetable. Facebook allows you to create a daily budget or a lifetime budget:

Daily Budget:
Choose Daily Budget if you want your ad to run indefinitely. Choose how much you're willing to pay per day on this specific ad. Remember that this is an average so that you may spend slightly more or less on some days.

Lifetime Budget:
Choose Lifetime Budget if you want to run your ad for a set period. Facebook will attempt to distribute the money you provide throughout the specified period evenly.

You may select the proper timetable for your ad set based on whatever option you select. Choose whether you want your advertising to begin immediately or at a later time.

Facebook Ad Formats

After you've chosen your campaign and ad set, it's time to develop your advertisements. First, you'll choose the format, media, content, and links for one or more advertisements in this area. Next, upload your creative materials and compose a clickable ad headline once you've decided how you want your ad to look. Facebook will make design suggestions for each format, including picture size, headline length, and other factors.

Previously, if an ad's picture had 20% or more text, Facebook would reject the ad. Facebook has recently implemented a new algorithm, although it still prefers photos with less text. Ads with more text will now receive less or no delivery at all. Use this tool to put your photos through their paces.

Finally, fine-tune your wording and test your ad on a desktop or mobile device. After that, place your order.

Measuring Facebook Ad Results

You'll want to keep an eye on how your ads perform now that they've been launched into the wild. Return to the Facebook Ad Manager to view the results. If you have advertisements running, you will get a list of all your campaigns.

The dashboard will provide an estimate of how much you spend on advertisements each day at the top. In addition, the dashboard is divided into columns to filter outcomes, reach easily, or money spent.

When assessing the performance of your advertising, there are several metrics to examine, such as reach, impressions, clicks, click-through rate, and more. First, however, there are a few things to keep in mind:

Actions: You choose an objective for your campaign in the first stage of generating a Facebook ad. When assessing the effectiveness of your campaign, keep your initial rationale in mind.

Cost per action: Don't simply look at the total number of activities. Examine the cost of each action and compare it to the cost of your other advertisements within the ad package.

Frequency: The frequency of your ad is the number of times it was seen. The optimal frequency should vary based on the sort of advertisement you run. For example, you would most likely want someone to see a promoted piece of information only once. However, it may take several views of a Page, Like an ad, before someone takes action. If one of your advertisements has a high frequency but a low performance, it may be time to retire.

Chapter-06: How to Create an Effective Facebook Marketing Strategy

It makes no difference the channel you choose; you must establish a strategy. This will assist you in clearly defining your goals, selecting the best tactics to achieve them, defining your target audience, measuring the performance of your efforts, and improving. We describe an approach that applies to every business looking to create a Facebook marketing strategy below.

1. Set your objectives.
2. Define your intended audience.
3. Select content types and publish pieces regularly.
4. Use Facebook Ads to promote your content.
5. Use Facebook's tools.
6. Assess your efficiency.

Step 1. Set your goals

It all starts with setting goals. The main aims for each firm are the same, regardless of the sort of business. Facebook provides possibilities to achieve the following objectives:

- generating leads;
- nurturing and qualifying your leads;

- driving traffic to a website;
- increasing conversions and sales;
- improving customer support;
- raising brand awareness;
- boosting customer engagement;
- recruitment.

The tactics, articles, and ad types you will employ to attain your aim are determined by your goal. You can divide your goal into smaller interim goals. As a result, completing each of them will get you closer to your ultimate goal. Finally, develop a list of key performance indicators (KPIs) that you will use to assess the efficacy of each approach.

Step 2. Define your target audience

Analyzing your target market is a high-priority assignment since it will influence the tactics, ad styles, and tone of voice you use. To begin, we recommend that you respond to the following questions:

- Is your product aimed at males or women?
- How old are your clients?
- What are their most prevalent occupations?
- What do they both have in common?
- What are the benefits of using your product?
- What are they hoping to achieve with it?

Create a customer profile to collect and save all of the data about your target audience and make the entire process more efficient. It should include information about their location, age, gender, employment title, and income level. Learn how to establish a customer profile by reading our blog post.

Facebook Audience Insights is another source of information about your target audience. This tool will provide you with information on individuals linked to your page, people in your custom audience, and people on Facebook. For example, you may learn about your current audience's preferences, where they reside and what language they speak, their previous purchase habits, the devices they use, and so on. This is a database containing information about your clients. Take advantage of every tool at your disposal to study your audience.

Step 3. Choose content formats and schedule posts

Now that you've identified your target audience and stated your objectives, it's time to devise a content strategy to assist you in reaching them. A content marketing strategy is developing a step-by-step plan covering the types and styles of content you will produce. Keep in mind that the more content you generate, the greater your conversion rate will be. Using various formats, posting consistently, and engaging with consumers will significantly increase your user engagement. You might also consider utilizing the appropriate content mix. Promotional material by itself will not assist you in developing trustworthy connections with your target audience.

Furthermore, Facebook can punish aggressive marketers for their sales advertisements. As a result, combine instructional, informative, entertaining, and promotional content. Customers will want to learn more about your product if you provide high-quality and relevant information.

Include the following information in your content marketing schedule to make it more effective:

- all the channels you use;
- the types of content you use;
- the date and time of publishing;
- the topic of your post;
- URL;
- the image link;
- the status of the post.

Fortunately, Facebook allows you to schedule posts and set up auto-publishing. As a result, there is no need to be concerned about any human errors.

Step 4. Boost your post with Facebook Ads

Facebook is a fantastic advertising tool. It enables companies to contact many people, offers a range of targeting choices, tools for effective outreach, and very affordable cost. Furthermore, it is built around a bidding technique. As a result, you have complete control over the time, ad placement, and target audience.

To begin designing your ad, navigate to the "Ad Center" and select "Create Ad."

The ad center's interface is straightforward so that you won't have any problems. However, it takes six steps to create an ad. To create your ad, follow this step-by-step tutorial.

Step 5. Make use of Facebook tools

Facebook offers far more value than you may anticipate. There are several tools available to help you make your work with this channel more successful and profitable. A list of some of the tools is provided below.

Facebook Messenger

It is an app designed to keep you in touch with your consumers through text messaging, video, and audio conversations. You may use this app to keep your audience engaged, create tailored experiences, and provide assistance. Delegate regular activities to a chatbot, such as managing orders and reservations, answering FAQs, and delivering vital information. Based on the buttons that your consumers click, you may create a flow. Text, pictures, product cards, galleries, files, lists, and other types can all be used. The message will be sent when a user inputs the term you selected when building the bot, such as "pricing," "delivery," "buy," "refund," and so on.

Follow these three simple steps to develop a Facebook Messenger chatbot:

- ✓ Connect your Send Pulse account to your Facebook profile.
- ✓ Choose a Facebook page.
- ✓ Make a widget to gather followers.

Pages to Watch

You may use this tool to assess your rivals' performance and follower engagement. Total page likes, publishing frequency, and growth rates may all be tracked. This knowledge will inspire you to grow and progress. In addition, you may examine your rivals' strategies to learning what they do better. To learn who your rivals are, go to the "Insights" area and scroll down to the "Pages to Watch" section. Add your competitors' pages and monitor their activity.

Invite Engaged Users

Some individuals may come across your postings and like or share them without being a fan. You may invite them to follow your brand personally. With a well-designed approach, you will interact with interested users and convert them into leads. Another way to improve group involvement is to send an invitation straight to your Messenger pals. When you click "Invite People," you may select friends from your list to like your page. If you activate this option, the invitation will be delivered immediately to Messenger. These are some of the useful tools provided by Facebook. You can get the most out of Facebook by thoroughly investigating the Ads Center choices and Insights capabilities.

Step 6: Measure your effectiveness

Your approach will not succeed on its own. Its effectiveness is largely determined by how effectively your target audience engages with your brand. Monitoring their interaction can provide you a clear image of which tactics perform best for you and which turn off your followers. Fortunately, you don't need to use any third-party services to track your effectiveness because Facebook has its tool called Insights. You'll learn which formats operate best and whether your content mix was properly prepared. You may monitor page visits, post interaction, story reach, page activities, evaluate your following, and more useful data. Use Google Analytics, UTM parameters, Hootsuite Insights, and other tools to measure conversions outside of Facebook, like reservations and transactions.

Conclusion

Naturally, you want your Facebook business Page to be a success. However, depending on your company goals, what success looks like on social media will differ. Your primary goal might be on launching new goods, increasing awareness, generating revenue, or gathering leads. But, in any case, you must like it. A "like" is how a person raises their hand and expresses their intent to receive updates from your company in their News Feed. If the long-term consequences of a low interaction rate aren't enough to terrify you, keep in mind that Facebook has a staff that monitors this type of questionable activity. They will not hesitate to deactivate your page without notice. Now that we've discussed how not to acquire likes, let's move on to obtaining them the proper way. We'll begin by advertising your Page on Facebook and then move on to your other marketing assets. When selecting connections, be wary of over-promotion to those you know will be uninterested. Spammy Facebook marketing is more harmful than beneficial. Don't forget to ask your coworkers to like your page as well. Encourage them to share it with their Facebook friends and add the unique link in their email signatures. Employees in sales, customer service, or human resources who routinely contact individuals outside your company are frequently a good match.

Finally, get involved. Building an engaged community is the greatest method to get Page likes. Share useful or interesting material with your followers that they will want to enjoy and share. Respond to messages as soon as possible, and interact with comments on your postings. Have you ever noticed that certain Pages have a green label that says they're "extremely receptive to messages"? You can get this badge if you have a 90% response rate and an average response time of fewer than 15 minutes in the past seven days. The promotion of your page does not end with Facebook. Are including social media follow buttons on your website and blog so that your audience can connect with you on Facebook easily.

www.ingramcontent.com/pod-product-compliance
Lightning Source LLC
Chambersburg PA
CBHW030038230526
45472CB00002B/574